WHAT IS TIME PRODUCTIVELY AND ITS BENEFITS?

Why is time usage significant in our daily Life?

By

Dr. Stella Martin

Table of Content

Introduction

Tolerating our mortality assists us with relinquishing hecticness and spotlight on what means a lot to us to carry on with a more joyful, more significant life.

The typical human life expectancy is ridiculously, startlingly limited. This reality, which a large portion of us disregard more often than not, is something to grapple with if we need to invest our restricted energy on this planet well.

Considering that, it follows that using time effectively, and comprehensively characterized, ought to be everybody's main concern. However, the advanced discipline of using time effectively (or efficiently) is depressingly intolerant, centered around formulating the ideal morning standard or attempting to wrench through whatever number of errands as could be expected under the circumstances, while money management uses all your energy on arriving at some later condition of prosperity and achievement. It overlooks the way that the world is overflowing with amazement — and that encountering a greater amount of that marvel might come at the expense of efficiency.

Part of that hug of limits includes confronting the nervousness that accompanies recognizing mortality. At the point when we perceive the brevity of life — and acknowledge the way that a few things must be left unaccomplished, regardless of whether we like it — we are more liberated to zero in on what is important. Instead of capitulating to the attitude of "better, quicker, more," we can embrace being defective, and be more joyful for it.

As a recuperating "efficiency nerd," I know how it feels to become cleared up in finding the ideal arrangement of using time effectively. However, I was ultimately compelled to acknowledge that my battles to accomplish a feeling of wonderful control or dominance over my time were counterproductive, driving not to the existence of really meaning but rather one of more overpowering and push. I came to see that I expected to surrender the mission for that sort of control, relinquishing the unimaginable objective of turning out to be entirely productive and embracing my restrictions, all things considered, to make additional opportunities for what was truly significant.

Chapter 1:
What is using Time Effectively?

Like our energy and cash, time is a limited asset and in that capacity, it should be successfully made due. Using time productively is tied in with arranging and controlling how much time you spend on unambiguous errands.

Using time effectively is the coordination of assignments and exercises to boost the viability of a singular's endeavors. Basically, the motivation behind using time effectively is empowering individuals to accomplish more and better work significantly quicker.

The five most significant time usage abilities are:

- Arranging.
- Navigation and prioritization.
- Defining limits and saying no.
- Appointing and reevaluating errands.
- Building a framework and tenaciously following it

Why using Time Productively is Significant in Business

The following are 10 ideas for Time Management for Mortals — and how to live in light of your restricted time.

1. Performing multiple tasks seldom functions admirably — and you'll before long find that serializing assists you with finishing more undertakings at any rate.
Take on a "fixed volume" way to deal with deficiency.
We as a whole need to pursue difficult decisions about what we can practically finish, so we can focus on the exercises that make the biggest difference, rather than responding to a steady flood of requests.

One way is to keep two daily agendas — one for everything on your plate, and one for the 10 or fewer things that you're as of now chipping away at. Top of the 10 openings on the second rundown with things from the first, then, at that point, set to work. The standard isn't to move any further things from the main run down onto the second until you've opened up space by completing one of the 10 things.

A connected technique is to set a pre-laid out time limit for specific kinds of day-to-day work — for instance, to set out to compose from 8 AM to 11 AM — and to ensure you stop when time's up.

2. Serialize
Center something like each large undertaking in turn. However it's charming to attempt to ease the uneasiness of having an excessive number of liabilities or aspirations by beginning on them at the same time, you'll gain little headway that way. Performing multiple tasks

4. Center around what you've as of how seldom functions admirably — and you'll before long find that serializing assists you with finishing more undertakings in any case, along these lines alleviating your tension.

3. Choose Ahead of Time what to fizzle at

You'll unavoidably underachieve at something, basically in light of the fact that your significant investment is limited. Be that as it may, key underachievement — choosing ahead of time the parts of your life in which you will not anticipate greatness — assists you with centering your significant investment all the more actually.
For instance, you could choose ahead of time that it's OK to have a jumbled kitchen while you finish your novel or to do the absolute minimum on a specific work project so you can invest more energy with your kids.

To experience this way is to trade the high-pressure mission for balance between fun and serious activities with something more sensible — a purposeful sort of irregularity.

finished, in addition to one side to do
Since the journey to finish, everything is wearisome by definition, it's not difficult to develop sorrowful and self-critical when you can't overcome your entire plan for the day. One counter-technique is to keep a "done list," which starts void first thing, but which you can continuously fill in over the course of the day as you finish things. It's a cheering update that you might have gone through the day doing nothing somewhat productive … yet you didn't.

5. Combine your mindful
Online entertainment is a goliath machine for inspiring you to invest your energy thinking often about some unacceptable things — and such a large number of them on the double. We're presented to a ceaseless stream of outrages and treacheries, every one of which could have a genuine case on our time and our magnanimous gifts, however which amount to something no human might at any point successfully address thoroughly.

When you embrace that reality completely, it's great to deliberately pick your fights in the foundation, activism, and governmental issues — and commit your extra time just to those particular causes. Center your ability for care, so you don't wear out.

6. Embrace exhausting and single-reason innovation

Computerized interruptions permit us to disappear to a domain where difficult human constraints don't appear to apply — looking over inactively around on the web, you really want never feel exhausted or obliged in your opportunity of activity, which isn't the situation with regards to taking care of business that is important.

You can battle this by making your gadgets as exhausting as could be expected, eliminating web-based entertainment applications and, if you think it wise, email. It's additionally useful to pick gadgets for only one reason, like the Kindle peruser. Any other way, enticements will be just a swipe away, and you'll want to check your screens whenever you're exhausted or confronting a test in your work.

7. Search out oddities in the ordinary

Time appears to accelerate as we age, logical on the grounds that our minds encode the entry of years in view of how much data we process in some random stretch. While youngsters have numerous clever encounters and time accordingly appears slower to them, the routinization of more established individuals' lives implies that time appears to elapse at an always expanding rate.

The standard counsel is to battle this by packing more original encounters into your life. That can help, yet entirely it's not commonsense 100% of the time.

An option is to focus harder on each second, but commonplace — to track down curiosity by diving all the more profoundly into your current life. Have a go at going on spontaneous strolls to see where they lead you, taking up drawing or bird watching or playing "I Spy" with a kid — whatever brings your consideration into the second more completely.

8. Be a researcher in relationships

The longing to feel in charge of our restricted time leads to various issues in connections, coming about in a controlling way of behaving, yet in addition to responsibility fear, the powerlessness to tune in, weariness, and passing up the wealth of common encounters with others.

When confronted with a difficult or exhausting second seeing someone, being interested in the individual you're with, instead of controlling. Interest is a position appropriate to the innate flightiness of existence with others, since it very well may be fulfilled by their conduct in manners you like or aversion — while in the event that you request a specific outcome all things being equal, you'll frequently be disappointed.

9. Develop momentary liberality

At the point when a liberal motivation emerges to you, yield to it immediately as opposed to putting it off. Try not to hold back to sort out whether or not the beneficiary merits your liberality or on the other hand assuming you have the opportunity to be liberal at the present time (with all of the work you have left to do!). Get it done. The prizes are prompt, as well, on the grounds that liberal activity dependably causes you to feel a lot more joyful.

10. Work on sitting idle

With regards to the test of utilizing your 4,000 weeks well, the ability to not do anything is crucial, since, supposing that you can't bear the distress of not acting, you're undeniably bound to pursue unfortunate decisions with your time, for example, endeavor to hustle exercises that can't be hurried or feeling you should spend each second being "useful," whether or not the undertakings being referred to truly matter.

Doing nothing implies fighting the temptation to control your experience or individuals and things in your general surroundings, and to leave things alone as they are. You can attempt the "sit idle" reflection, where you set a clock for 5-10 minutes and afterward have a go at sitting idle. On the off chance that you find yourself following through with something — thinking, say, or even zeroing in on your breath — tenderly let go of making it happen.

As you continue to give up, you'll expand your capacity to sit idle and steadily recapture your independence. You'll never again be so roused by the endeavor to dodge how reality feels at this very moment; all things considered, you'll figure out how to quiet down and pursue better decisions with your short assignment of life.

Chapter 2

How to Help a Representative Who Battles with Using time productively

The indications are there: Undertakings did without a second to spare, finished late, or even neglected. Lateness at gatherings. No reaction to messages or answers at bizarre times, Furthermore, more clarification of why things aren't finished than an activity to complete them.

You have an immediate report battling with using time productively. As a director, it very well may be trying to know how to resolve the issue. From one perspective, you really want them to finish things, and your normal propensity can be to answer in a clear disturbance at the absence of finish or even to think about thinking of them up. Then again, you need to foster your colleagues. You might have really splendid people who you know can possibly be uncommon supporters on the off chance that they could sort out some way to actually utilize their time.

As a time usage mentor, I talk with individuals who battle in this space consistently. I know how their cerebrums work, and I assist them with moving into a position of more significant levels of efficiency.

On the off chance that you're a supervisor uncertain of how to help, here are a few viable advances you can take to advance the circumstance, beginning today.

Recognize your own feelings.

On the off chance that you've been dealing with this individual for quite a while, you've probably encountered an expansive scope of feelings going from gentle disturbance to by and large infuriation. Your sentiments will change contingent upon how serious the issues have been, the stakes in question, your character, your assumptions, and your feelings of anxiety.

Before you give criticism to your representative, recognize your own feelings. Work out whatever you could be thinking or feeling in a free-stream way. Try not to share your crude contemplations (by means of email etc.) with your associate. This exercise is so you can become mindful of your own inward state.

Process what you're feeling all alone or with a confided face-to-face and genuinely survey for what reason you're so vexed. Is it an absence of control? Shame? Stress?

Pinpoint the pressure.

Recently, I had what was happening I saw as exceptionally upsetting with an external project worker. There was an enormous venture that I wanted them to finish, and they were exceptionally deferred. One day as I was mulling over everything, I understood that inside the bigger undertaking, there were only several particular things that made the biggest difference. Whenever those were finished, my pressure would decisively diminish, and different parts could take additional time.

By explaining my most significant requirements, I felt considerably less focused on and could convey what I expected to get back most critically, regardless of whether the entire task wasn't finished.

Set aside some margin to thoroughly consider precisely the exact thing causing issues for you with your immediate report's absence of using time productively: Do you not have what you really want for significant update gatherings or introductions? Could it be said that you are encountering pressure from them requesting that you survey things last moment? Are their activities costing you time or cash? Do you feel restless when there's bad correspondence on status? When you know this, it will assist with centering your criticism conversations.

Impart what you want.

When you know precisely the exact thing's annoying you, smoothly convey precisely the exact thing you really want, when you want it, and why you want it. You can likewise ask them what they need from you to assist them with finding success.

In spite of the fact that you might feel enticed to dump all of your disappointment on your immediate report about the pressure they've caused you and the issues they've had, a brutal methodology will regularly misfire. They'll be so wrecked by your displeasure and shut down or become guarded and stall. Take full breaths, and attempt to recall that they probably have good intentions however basically battle around here.

Help toward the beginning.

In certain circumstances, basically giving criticism about what you want or need can advance the circumstance. However, in others, you'll have to accomplish other things to assist things with pushing ahead.

To kick your immediate report off, think about making these moves with them:

Get some margin to thoroughly consider precisely the exact thing causing issues for you with your immediate report's absence of using time productively: Do you not have what you want for significant update gatherings or introductions? Is it true or not that you are encountering pressure from them requesting that you audit things last moment? Are their activities costing you time or cash? Do you feel restless when there's bad correspondence on status? When you know this, it will assist with centering your input conversations.

Convey what you want.

When you know precisely very thing's annoying you, serenely impart precisely exact thing you really want, when you want it, and why you This interaction assists you with delivering repressed pessimistic feelings before you give input so that you're not excessively cruel with your immediate report and cause more damage than great.

Your immediate report might just have unfortunate using time productively. Yet, you should consider whether you likewise have unfortunate time usage abilities and in which ways, if any, you're adding to the issue.

In the event that you send over tasks without a second to spare, don't provide clear guidance, decline to lay out boundaries, have no subsequent framework, or neglect to give criticism, then, at that point, your activities could be assuming a part in the circumstance. In the event that you additionally anticipate that your representatives should be continually accessible through email, talk, or different channels, so they can't define limits to finish centered work, you're likewise somewhat to blame for the battles they face.

By distinguishing these issues ahead of the critical discussion, you can join recognize where you could likewise have improved.
Despite the fact that you might feel enticed to dump all of your dissatisfaction on your immediate report about the pressure they've caused you and the issues they've had, an unforgiving methodology will regularly misfire. They'll be so wrecked by your indignation and shut down or become cautious and stall. Take full breaths, and attempt to recollect that they probably have good intentions however basically battle around here.

- Work with them to focus on the work
- Conceptualize the bearing to take
- Talk through the more modest parts
- Set up halfway achievements
- Do a portion of the work with them in a gathering
- Group them up with partners
- Demand every day updates on what they wanted to do and what they've achieved

Organizing what is happening with the goal that they can get and keep force can improve things greatly.

Value progress.

At the point when you begin seeing development in the correct bearing, show appreciation for each step in the right direction. You might feel worried that giving good input excessively fast when they haven't done all that yet will make them slack off. Yet, the inverse is normally evident. Positive criticism assists with building their certainty, inspiration, and inspiration and can drive them toward endlessly improved results.

Your immediate report probably realizes they have genuinely awful using time productively and may have a more regrettable outlook on it than you do. Laying into them is counterproductive; expanded pessimistic feelings about their work for the most part creates more setbacks, not less. Recall that you're in the same boat. Rather than destroying them, develop them at every turn.

Get outside help.

Once in a while, you're excessively near a circumstance. Regardless of how diligently you attempt, you can't give evenhanded, quiet criticism. Or on the other hand, your immediate report will be unable to be straightforward with you about what's genuinely happening, for example, squandering hours every day looking on their telephone or a circumstance at home that might be diverting them.

In these circumstances, it very well may be useful to associate your worker with outside assets, for example, time usage preparing, an inside mentor, or an outer mentor who can assist them with fostering these abilities. Somebody with experience in assisting individuals with conquering these difficulties and who is all the more genuinely far off from the circumstance can frequently be more successful than somebody with a background marked by disappointment.

As a director, you can't compel anybody to further develop their use time effectively. However, your correspondence and activities can have a tremendous effect on your immediate report's capacity to defeat their battles and increment their efficiency.

Chapter 3.

What Reason do so many Entrepreneurs Hesitate?

Put pen to paper to visualize just what can get done each day.

Business visionaries are famously overstretched and limited capacity to focus pack. They succeed at covering themselves in everyday business happenings to the impediment of such significant long-haul errands as accounting and long-haul arranging. Furthermore, care and taking care of. Include family responsibilities and side interests, and planning gets tangled — quick. Time usage master Marydee Sklar, the proprietor of authoritative preparation organization Leader Working Achievement, assists entrepreneurs with arranging beneficially. She shared her tips in a meeting, which have been altered for length and lucidity:

It resembles a riddle where you have these open spaces and you pick your undertakings to fill them. Today, I had a hole of 15 minutes before my client appeared, and I thought: "What's on my plan for the day that will fit?" So your daily agenda isn't a rundown, however, relegated seasons of 10 or 30 or an hour, and you plan spatially by thinking, "Where could the right space of time for me to do this undertaking be?"

Many bobs around without finishing responsibilities, and afterward things fire stacking up — and they begin to drop balls, get overpowered, and vanish from doing what they should do.

The issue with time is that it's theoretical. You can't see or contact it, so you must think of a substantial framework that keeps your time and errand before you. I'm a colossal defender of paper. I consider it supporting your cerebrum with a spot to offload and hold everything — and access it rapidly.

Google Schedule is awesome for arrangements. I was unable to live without it — however not really for arranging. On a screen, you can't get a sufficiently large perspective on the future, and afterward, you change to another capability, and everything vanishes. This truly doesn't work for pioneering-type individuals, who frequently can't hold everything.

They frequently do "horrible" errands, which is concluding that an undertaking will require some investment and be upsetting, so they can't begin it now. They additionally hopefully believe that time is stretchy.

Is there a response?

I call it being a period researcher. You record what amount of time it requires for you to do ordinary undertakings that you despise doing. For instance, I discovered that signing into my financial balance to set aside installments and move cash around requires just shy of 15 minutes. So I did that during my 15-minute hole toward the beginning of today.

How might business people focus on their tasks?

Well-being is the principal thing on your daily agenda. Assuming you go down, the entire business goes down, so focus on exercise and dealing with yourself. I exercise and deal with myself toward the beginning of the day.

What comes straightaway?

No. 2 is any assignment associated with cash. Cash causes pressure and tension, and it'll surprise you and stack up. Many individuals stow away from cash, and afterward, they don't use sound judgment.

Also, need No. 3?

Extinguishing fires — like the site's down. And afterward from that point forward, you focus on what on your rundown will help you later on, and fit in those future errands.

Do you do yearly preparation?

We plunk down consistently, and I put in the entirety of my cutoff times for our items, administrations, courses, and advertising. The principal thing I do is invested get-away effort. That is something business visionaries won't ever do.

Chapter 4

Why using time Effectively is Significant for Students

Successful using time productively permits understudies to finish more significantly quicker, on the grounds that their consideration is engaged and they're not squandering life on interruptions (like web-based entertainment, for instance. Effective utilization of time likewise diminishes pressure, as understudies tick off things from their daily agenda.

Why using Time Productively is Significant in Understudy

A portion of the significant abilities understudies need to oversee time successfully include:

1. Objective setting

It's exceedingly difficult to utilize time well in the event that you don't have any idea how to manage it. Understudies can profit from having short-and long haul objectives. For instance, a transient objective could incorporate finishing their schoolwork early every day, so they have adequate opportunity to rehearse music. Their drawn-out objective could be to play in the everyday schedule band or the Australian Youth Symphony!

2. Prioritization

By surveying what should be accomplished within a given time span, undertakings can be evaluated by their significance. Laying out boundaries for every day, week, month and year can assist understudies with achieving their objectives. It additionally assists with guaranteeing exercises that are essentially significant yet not critical - like individual dedications, satisfactory rest, and exercise - are given priority. Certain
Certain sports, leisure activities, youth gatherings, and investing energy with loved ones.

Great using time effectively permits understudies to take full advantage of their capacities and partake in the fulfillment of achievement. It is additionally one of the best abilities for business.

The Holy book likewise has a great deal to say regarding dealing with our time. Christians make various memories and points of view to the world - we realize we are essential for God's timeless arrangement of salvation through Christ Jesus (Eph 1:4).

Therefore, we really want to guarantee our needs are right, by looking for first His realm and honorableness (Matt 6:33). We are told to utilize our time astutely (Eph 5:15-17), and to look for God's insight about how best to do this (Ps 90:12). We are urged to make arrangements for the future (Prov 21:5) however keep them in offset with realizing they aren't ensured (Js 4:13-14).

Focusing our eyes on the everlasting point of view (2 Cor 4:18) will prompt time usage that lauds God and assists us with the live excursion of His will.

Tips on how to Improve Time Management

Luckily, there are numerous ways understudies can further develop their use time effectively. Here is a broad rundown, got from locales including Level Power Learning and Deakin College.

Begin with a plan - either alone or with your assistance, have your kid record the dates of every forthcoming task and test in a web or paper plan (like their school journal or an internet-based schedule). Plan for significant exercises and extra energy, as well. You could in fact set cutoff times a couple of days before real due dates to permit an edge for crises.

Make an expert timetable - from this plan, close off pieces of time for study or task work. This will assist your understudy with focusing on their ventures and remaining on track with due dates. You could begin by assessing what amount of time each undertaking will require, then, at that point, ascertain how long to permit day to day or week after week. Attempt to plan for some concentration consistently day, regardless of whether it's just short. Variety coding of various subjects can make perusing the timetable simpler.

Begin tasks early - leaving tasks as late as possible is upsetting. All things considered, urge your kid to begin dealing with them a long time before they are expected.

Make project arrangements - when study or tasks appear to be overpowering, tarrying frequently results. Assist your youngster with breaking their review plan or undertaking into more modest, more sensible pieces. You can give each portion its own due date to assist them with feeling better about meeting little objectives.

Keep away from performing multiple tasks - separated consideration is a wasteful method for learning. Center around each assignment in turn for the most extreme efficiency.

Diminish interruptions - during time booked for homework, have your youngster take care of superfluous gadgets like cell phones, and switch off virtual entertainment warnings. Interruptions can likewise come from inside sentiments like appetite or sluggishness, so guarantee they're getting sufficient rest and have bites and water available.

Enjoy customary reprieves - chipping away at something for a really long time can prompt lost center. Brief breaks each half hour or so can assist them with re-energizing. Consider having a difference in the scene, like a short walk or a beverage on the lawn. Simply ensure they don't get diverted and don't get back to study!

Be a morning person - urge your kid to begin their schoolwork as soon as conceivable after school. This gives them additional opportunity to finish it while they're ready and diminishes the gamble of postponed sleep times. Likewise, individuals change with regards to when they're generally useful, so permit your understudy to handle testing undertakings during their best time, and leave simpler ones, (for example, arranging their books or records for the following day) when they're not at their pinnacle. Some could like to rise and shine early and work before the school day, for instance.

Furthermore, here are a few additional valuable tips from Psych Focal, Trick of the trade, and The Equilibrium Vocations.

Set time limits -, for example, "finish Prologue to Humanities paper by 3.30 pm". This forestalls assignments eating into time apportioned for different exercises. Use time following applications and programming, for example, those recorded here on Trick of the trade.

Keep a clock put noticeably before you - to remain mindful of the current time.

Keep away from compulsiveness and getting all worked up about irrelevant subtleties - attempting to make your work great, particularly first-time round, is baffling and a gigantic time-squanderer. Rather, get something on the page (or into the cerebrum). You can return and further develop it later if fundamental.

Utilize your personal time well - for instance, understudies could be practicing their times' tables or rehearsing an oral show in the vehicle en route to or from school. On an open vehicle, they might have the option to study or thoroughly consider their arrangement for that day.

This tip ought to be utilized with shrewdness and balance, however, as time for unwinding and rest is additionally fundamental.

Reward accomplishment - when your youngster has achieved significant objectives, remember to celebrate. This doesn't need to be something significant or costly. Ideally, it ought to be a solid thing. Conceivable outcomes incorporate some additional gadget or television time, a visit to a most loved ocean side, park or movement, a little treat, or even a commitment towards something they are putting something aside for.

Is it conceivable to be throughout fanatical no time like the present administration?

Empowering kids to deal with their time well is reasonable, yet it's additionally feasible for over-the-top using time productively to be counterproductive. Consistently looking for ways of utilizing time all the more successfully can leave kids feeling more restless and pushed.

As per this BBC article, the accessible proof recommends that time usage apparatuses and techniques work for certain individuals in certain conditions, yet for nobody else. Covering 2017 exploration, they note that constantly pursuing better using time productively turns into a foolish methodology, in which individuals can at first complete more by utilizing these devices, yet fail to remember the way that efficiency has limits.

A more serious result happens when individuals neglect to focus on their genuine inspirations. This is one of the principal motivations behind why such strategies fall flat, said Christine Carter, a senior individual at UC Berkeley's More prominent Great Science Community. Many of them depend on self-discipline for progress, yet "you are not exactly persuaded by resolution as much as by your inclination."

Brad Age, one of the review's creators, calls attention to the that individuals today typically have extensively more opportunities to sort out their time and are shuffling numerous tasks, which causes a great deal of tension. "Opportunity accompanies an obligation: you need to think significantly more about how you deal with your time," he says.

He had something of a revelation subsequent to thinking about that we will pass on, and it changed his time usage reasoning. He presently wakes every day at 9 am following a nine-hour rest, labors for four hours out each day, goes to the exercise center, and understands day to day. He utilizes a few time usage procedures, including plans for the day, schedules, and clocks, however not stuff his existence with work. According to rather,, these devices "ought to permit you to assume command over your life, and afterward structure your work around it".

In a culture that frequently makes an icon of hecticness, this is a significant wake-up call about existence's motivation and needs. God implores us to trust Him to accommodate our requirements, not fill our days with anxious endeavoring (Matt 6:25-34).

Chapter 5

The benefit of Time Management

Given the restricted measure of time you have in a day, you need to capitalize on it. It's not difficult to become with free-for-all exercises and accomplish less. Here are more motivations behind why dealing with your time in school is fundamental:

What are the Benefits of Time Management for Students?

- It assists you with accomplishing your objectives quicker. ...
- It Assists you with focusing on your work. ...
- You accomplish more significantly quicker. ..
  Lessens pressure. ...
- Forestalls are stalling. ...
- It supports your certainty and offers . . . .
- Further developed professions have valuable open doors. ...
- Characterize and focus on your undertakings. ...
- Separate undertakings into more modest errands.

1. It assists you with accomplishing your objectives quicker

Appropriate time usage makes you more powerful. Rather than becoming involved with performing multiple tasks, you center around each action in turn for a predefined length. Along these lines, you do the best that you can with it, which brings about you accomplishing your objectives quicker. For example, to work on your grades in a particular subject, at the Worldwide Indian Global School opening in an additional opportunity to deal with it will assist you with raising your grades quicker.

2. It Assists you with focusing on your work.

While making a period table, you focus on fundamental errands that require prompt activity. For example, finishing your tasks precedes a review meeting or study bunch. With legitimate using time effectively, you can open so as to chip away at your tasks prior to going for a review bunch. This implies that you can get done with fundamental responsibilities on time since you can plan and make opportunities to chip away at them.

3. You accomplish more significantly quicker

Dispensing a particular errand at its own time assists you with zeroing in on it more. By adhering to this time plan, you have a superior possibility of handling the undertaking than getting to it with no predefined time designated to it. Take finishing tasks or dealing with an undertaking. In the event that you don't devote time to chip away at them, you will probably neglect to finish them. Having a legitimate timetable permits you to dispense sufficient opportunity to each errand to hit your cutoff times in time.

4. Lessens pressure

You can immediately end up being focused on in the event that you have a considerable rundown of activities and not sufficient opportunity to finish them. Appropriately using time productively empowers you to focus on and tackle assignments first. Along these lines, you know precisely the exact thing you want to do and how long you need to finish each job. This diminishes your nervousness and by and large pressure since you have sufficient opportunity to finish everything.

5. Prevents Procrastination

Stalling is a dangerous incline that prompts pressure, dissatisfaction, and low grades. Saving a predefined time for an undertaking gives you the inspiration you want to make it happen. It assists you with beating apathy which frequently adds to delay. Legitimate using of time effectively likewise permits you to designate sufficient opportunity to investigate or find support to handle the assignment. Not knowing how to handle a task is among the most widely recognized motivations behind why numerous Students tarry.

6. It helps your certainty and offers Further developed vocation potential open doors

Dealing with your time well permits you to finish your work on time. This evokes a feeling of certainty and achievement in your capacities. Getting past a long plan for the day can likewise inspire these sentiments, and it can act as an inspiration to further develop your time usage abilities. Mastering legitimate time usage abilities can help you outside school, also. At the point when you get utilized, it can assist you with turning into a solid representative who turns in devoted, great work on time. This works on your worth as a representative raising your expert standing, and opening up additional valuable chances to additional your profession.

[illegible]

[illegible]

[illegible]

Chapter 6

What is the Significance of Time Usage For Online Students?

Using time effectively Quite possibly the most important ability, you can have as an internet-based understudy is viable using time effectively. The better you deal with your time, the more straightforward it is to accomplish your objectives. Everybody has similar 24 hours in a day, meaning, there's really no need to focus on how long you have, yet the way in which well you can oversee it.

This is particularly significant for online students, who are in many cases working all day, dealing with family, or shuffling different responsibilities. Without the brotherhood of a class to propel you or making some set memories where you should be nearby, powerfully is critical to assisting you with remaining on track.

Compelling time usage assists with your advancement as well as make you more useful at work and in your own life. In the event that you're significant about effectively finishing your web-based degree, it's essential to track down a decent framework to utilize.

The following are seven-time usage tips to assist you with remaining in front of your coursework.

For students who are new to web-based learning, similar to those impacted by school terminations because of the Coronavirus pandemic or those essentially hoping to roll out an improvement, changing to internet learning can take some becoming accustomed to. Furthermore, on the off chance that you are changing in accordance with a full-time web-based program or adjusting to school and work, it is basic to have the option to really deal with your time.

Whether you've decided to seek internet learning or you've been pushed into it, there are key abilities you should make the most out of your web-based training, including using time productively.

Time Usage Tips for Online Understudies

1. Prepare.

Your rushed timetable joined with everyday interruptions, can undoubtedly hinder completing responsibilities. The best web-based understudies know how to make opportunities center. This incorporates making some steady memories and work area, blocking out those interruptions, and trying not to ride the web.

Regardless of the adaptability in being a web-based understudy, having a continuous commitment to your examinations all through the week is significant. Give a lot of chances to scatter your necessary readings, tasks, and online conversations.

Consider buying a schedule you can use to design your every day and week-after-week tasks, featuring:

Tasks due, including drafts and last entries

Exercises connected with your program, for example, concentrate on a bunch of meetups or nearby systems administration occasions

Virtual or in-person available time with teachers and consultants

Melanie Kasparian, partner head of evaluation for the Northeastern College School of Expert Investigations, shares an example timetable of what an ordinary week could resemble:

- Monday Start required readings and media
- Tuesday - Keep surveying materials
- Wednesday - Post to conversation gathering and start tasks
- Thursday - Keep posting and chipping away at tasks

- Friday - Read and answer posts and work on tasks
- Saturday - Read and answer posts and finish tasks
- Sunday - Actually take a look at your work and submit tasks

2. Don't perform various tasks.

Stay away from performing various tasks — which can really diminish your efficiency. Center around each task in turn and focus on the particular main job, whether that is reading up for a test, perusing a course book, messaging a teacher, or partaking in a web-based gathering. Organize your undertakings arranged by significance, and focus on the three or four critical assignments that require the most exertion.

In the event that you really want assistance remaining on track, consider making records utilizing a venture the board device, like Trello or Smartsheet, to assist with coordinating undertakings. On the off chance that you favor a customary plan for the day, take a gander at computerized scratch pads like Todoist, ClickUp, or Evernote.

Ultimately, focus on the main priority in the present and keep away from anything excessively far-off. In the event that it's a little task that you don't have to address for a long time, put it on your schedule to zero in on when the cutoff time is nearer.

3. Set up your virtual office.

Whether you learn at home or in your neighborhood bistro, it's essential to work in the ideal setting expected to finish your work. Ensure there's a rapid web, and that you're in an agreeable space with the right lighting, sound, and foundation. For instance, certain individuals like to work with

earphones on, while others favor quietness or a surrounding setting with individuals unobtrusively talking. Sit in an agreeable seat, and ensure the lighting isn't excessively faint. Close out your program windows, and set your telephone aside.
Alongside these components, ensure you have every one of the necessary materials, like course books and industry-explicit programming. Set up however much you can early on to keep focused on your coursework.

4. Shut out interruptions.
Make a point to try not to ride the web unnecessarily. It's not difficult to become diverted by the news or your #1 superstar tattle site. Remain on track, and stay away from Facebook, Twitter, and other web-based entertainment apparatuses when you want to focus on your examinations.

On the off chance that you're battling to keep on track, think about the Pomodoro Technique. This strategy assists with efficiency by organizing how you work to increment effectiveness. The device expands on 25-minute work meetings, streamlining your chance to zero in on your web-based examinations. The most effective way to utilize this technique is to:

Set a clock for 25 minutes and turn it out continuously for the booked period.
Require a five-minute break to snatch an espresso, browse messages, or accomplish something different.
Whenever you've finished four work meetings, indulge yourself with a more extended, 15-minute break.
In the event that you're actually battling with tarrying, download a site blocker for your Pomodoro meetings. Opportunity, KeepMeOut, and Trick limit web-based perusing and allow you to completely finish your everyday undertakings. With these devices, you can impede all sites or divert your number one locales to your school's landing page.

5. Reward yourself

It's vital to compensate yourself after nicely done to stay balanced. If not, focusing on even the most straightforward tasks will be troublesome.

You can remunerate yourself by praising your achievements and indulging yourself with something you really appreciate, whether that is watching your #1 show on Netflix or going out to a pleasant supper and a film. In the event that you've been dealing with a task for quite some time, then go home for the week when you're done.

6. Make an equilibrium.

As well as remunerating yourself, it's likewise essential to track down a harmony among coursework and your different commitments, particularly on the off chance that you're shuffling school and work.

To assist with making a compelling equilibrium and abstain from wearing out, make certain to focus on your time in a manner that permits you to zero in on school, work, and your own life as needed. Making an anticipated timetable can assist you with getting into a standard that works for your way of life and permits you to commit your complete focus to every part of your life at a given time.

7. Get a decent night's rest.

Rest is crucial for resting your body and keeping your psyche new for the following day. Attempt to get seven to eight hours of rest an evening. Pulling dusk 'til dawn affairs is less useful than concentrating reliably. Remember to rest for your timetable, and you can receive enormous benefits.

Assuming responsibility for Your Internet-based Training

Signing up for a web-based degree program is an extraordinary method for facilitating your schooling and at last development in your vocation, yet it really depends on you to assume responsibility for your advancement so you can capitalize on your classes. A critical part of doing so is utilizing viable time usage systems to keep steady over your obligations.
However significant as it very well might be to be a decent student, finding a web-based program that meets your requirements is likewise basic to progress. While picking a web-based degree program, make certain to do all necessary investigation and comprehend how the substance and construction of the courses line up with your own objectives and goals. In the event that professional success is your definitive objective, for instance, a program that values joint effort and systems administration could be a solid match.

By picking the right program to meet your requirements and assuming responsibility for your learning, you can set yourself up for internet learning achievement…..

IN CONCLUSION:

No matter how we divide it up, there are only 24 hours in a day, and managing them is necessary if we want to be efficient and productive in our work lives and feel energetic and happy personality, something that increases our quality of life.

The so-called time management refers to the way in which each one organizes and plans how much time they invest in specific activities. Spending more hours in the company does not mean being more efficient or productive. Therefore, proper time management in everything we are doing is essential. And it makes us sound healthy and live long.

www.ingramcontent.com/pod-product-compliance
Lightning Source LLC
LaVergne TN
LVHW020528160826
845677LV00015B/3967

* 9 7 9 8 8 4 2 7 3 4 5 8 0 *